I0210821

The De-Peopling Affair

The De-Peopling Affair

By Virginia Archer

Virginia Archer Publishing
2024

Copyright © 2024 by Jean Mederick

All rights reserved. This book or any portion thereof may not be reproduced or used in any manner whatsoever without the express written permission of the publisher except for the use of brief quotations in a book review or scholarly journal.

First Printing: 2024

ISBN 978-976-96004-5-4

Virginia Archer Publishing
P.O. Box 954
Castries, LC04 101
Saint Lucia
https://www.instagram.com/virginia.archer.poetry/

Front cover art by Jean Mederick ©

Back cover art by Jean Mederick ©

Ordering Information:
Special discounts are available on quantity purchases by corporations, associations, educators, and others. For details, contact the publisher at the above listed address.

U.S. trade bookstores and wholesalers: Please contact
Virginia Archer Publishing
Tel: (1758) 4841352 or email: virginia.archer.poetry@gmail.com

Dedication

I couldn't do this without the tribe; I love you.

Love to my daughter; she makes me want to do better.

the mosquito net
flickers like a ghost
backlit by the television
as i tiptoe over the sleeping dog
pick up my dormant phone
burn my eyes with the screen
begin to type the day to you
about how all i wanted to do today
was run
bury myself against the drum beat
in your chest
feel your arms fold me into shape
remould me
from falling apart
into strung together
pick up all my pieces
my depression from the floor
tell it to be quiet
hush
shhhhhhh

i type
and don't press send

I'VE CONVINCED MYSELF YOU'RE WORTHY OF POETRY, EVEN THOUGH I KNOW BETTER

I bit down hard on the corner of your shoulder
as if marking your flesh with the sentences
of my breaths,
marking you with last night's poem,
would somehow make you mine

but you were never one
to let sentiment sit on your skin too long

you once told me that you didn't like saying
I love you
too often
just in case it grew stale
on your lips

so I should have known
when you suddenly said the words
my parched soul longed for
that it was only your guilty conscience
reaching for salvation

but I'll write you another poem anyway
leave it in the sun to fade
like all the others

you were a page turner darling
all licked fingers
and fast paced words

i didn't see the cliffhanger
until that final page

and i hated the ending

I COULD RUIN THIS WITH JUST ONE DAMN BAD CLICHE

i tell myself it's just a quick note
a text message
that extends through the phone
carrying pieces of me

i ask
you respond
you affirm
and i try not to make a big deal out of crumbs
try to keep things casual

and all the while
everything i've been wanting to say
gets ice jammed in my throat
the words
backing up on each other
a car crash pile up of sentences

"see you later"
is all my texting fingers
can muster
while my head
screams every cringe worthy thing
i want to say
insert cliche here

and i wait for my heart
to stop thrashing like a trapped rabbit
deep in my chest

every little damn word between us
weighs a ton

LOVE IS ALL STOMACH PAIN AND DEAD BUTTERFLIES

I've been asking myself
why I can't just be honest
open my throat
and let all these butterflies
that have been flapping their last in my stomach
fly out in a cloud of I love you
beat their wings
against the curve of your lips
until you taste them
let them disintegrate on your tongue
a delicate heaviness
a bouquet heady with all these notes

my friends think I'm crazy
tell me to write it all down instead
ball it up
set it on fire

but I'm not sure
if I sent you a smoke signal
if I set the world aflame
you would notice

so I swallow the butterflies
hold them tight
in the ulcerated fist of my gut
and let the acid eat them alive

I WANT TO TASTE MORE THAN WORDS FROM YOUR MOUTH

you string your words so carefully
beautiful pearls;
i'd like to think my skin
could hold them as a benediction
the melanin of my breasts
rising to cup them
the cafe latte swirl of the continents of my flesh
be enough
that i could differentiate
between a blessing
and the stale words
of a regurgitated sermon
from three Sundays ago
from a decade ago

but every time
you say i'm beautiful
those words burn prayers
into my eyes
so i can't see myself anymore
and blinkered
the only thing that's straight ahead
is you

so don't call me beautiful
unless your hands are willing
to unbind the years we lost
lay them at my feet
and let me cross every stretch of this lake
my tears left between us

don't call me beautiful
unless you mean it

the smile cracked in my jaw last week
that last one i plastered on
right before you left

i guess the mask is slipping;
my bones have been holding you for so long
the osteoporosis of a decade
has eroded every ounce
of this bone marrowed love
into dust

the arthritic sob
of my hollowed out ribs
is letting you go

I'm Not Sure If Either One Of Us Can Remember How To Let Go

we forgot to have an ending

we've been chasing the tail
of this love
like lost puppies
round and round
until we're sick

you test me,
see if i still feel
the burn of your gaze
watch my skin react to your smile

but all the while
i feel like you're holding me at arms length
fingers round the velvet of my throat
choking off *i love yous*
as you observe my blue lips
hanging me over the edge
of perhaps
and maybe

so are we done?
or aren't we?

I WONDER IF YOU CAN FEEL ME BETWEEN HEARTBEATS

I have a friend who once said
that if you ever came back to me
all of the autoimmune stutters in my bones
would quit fluttering,
the pain of the weight of love
would move from crushing my spine
and tumble out of my mouth
and for one or more spectacular moments
perhaps I could breathe again
not need the crutch of drugs

so does that make you an obsession
or merely a disease?
is the cure
wedged between your teeth,
is *I love you*
all the panacea these aches need?

but while I wait
on a seeming answer
that you can't seem to spit,
my flesh wanders my skeleton
looking for the last imprints of your fingers
until I realize
you took the last ones with you
and my skin
looks so grey and meaningless
when my soul
is still lost in your ribs.

His eyes were black as night, a moonless pool
I could not see the depths, and yet I swam
I plunged into that night, a breathless fool
and sank into the dark, gave all I am
and there the waters drew me in, I drowned
within his gaze, he robbed me of my breath
and there and then my heart it became bound
and all else fell away, a sudden death.
I loved him then, my heart beat in his chest
no longer mine, my ribs an empty cage
my heart a bird, had found a place to rest
and I was lost, forever and an age.
I love him still, I take a nightly swim
within the eyes that fill me to the brim.

IF I COULD I WOULD BREAK EVERY BONE IN SEARCH OF YOU

i try to unlock the cage of my ribs;
but the key is rusted
around your name
in my heart

I'm A Botticelli Nude Hidden Under All These Scars

my words do a strip tease
along my tongue

i spit them out
into the palm of the paper
and watch them make a poem

heart line
life line
love lines
they criss cross
this space
my hand becomes frantic
waving
bare

i drown
between the distance of your heartbeats
and mine
swallowing water

but you don't open these sentences
and marvel at the skin
this tattooed landscape
of your name

and i dwell in my naked shame

this engine heart
under the rusted hood of these ribs
still beats
though these hands
these lips
are slower in the formation of words
though the divorce
of our skin
lies fragile and dented
between our sentences
under the stains
beneath all the dust
of the rain stained roads
we've cried
I think I love you,
somehow
still

stunning
the way the breath of your fingers
catches my thigh
and chases waves
into my throat,
my breath
a stutter
trying your name,   barely

THERE'S SO MUCH BEAUTY IN ALL THE PAINFUL THINGS

my bones
straddle the continents
between the air raid shelter
of my mother's English garden ribs
and the sugarcane beating scar
on my father's left brow

between the grey
old tooth boards
of Ma Zine's grin
and the loud drunken
laugh of the larger than life grandmother
I have tucked
in the back of my throat

and I watch
the earthquake beauty
of all the clashing plates
in my daughter's face
and know
I wouldn't change a thing

JUST LIKE THE DOVE (COUPLET SONNET)

The dove still coos at noon his mourning song
that echoes in the trees, and all along
the other birds will listen, cock each head
and when the words are weighty, wings are spread
for bluest skies where floating clouds of white
embrace each one within their soaring flight
and let them shed their cares along the breeze
above the waves of gently rocking seas
but still the mourning dove professes pain
with every song his breast it will contain
for love is lost somewhere among the leaves
of all the nodding, swaying, silent trees.
I mourn you now, just like the calling dove
I want your warmth, your arms, your eyes, your love.

I'll write a hymn about your eyes
about your teasing hands
a litany along my flesh
where touches become brands

this blasphemy of aching lips
the church within my chest
that know the arch of all your bones
beneath your beating breast

I stutter step along your spine
my fingers know your skin
and tattoo songs of ache and joy
of love and pain and sin

And you will sing my name to me
a groan into my ear
and I will pray against your mouth
so only we can hear.

WE SHOULD JUST SAY IT OUT LOUD WHILE WE CAN

I tucked new year's resolutions
into the pit of my stomach
and tried to hold on to
the last image of your smile
etched on the back of my eyes
with sunburst fireworks

but the year
broke like a fragile eggshell tsunami
in my hands

I guess I held your name
too long between my teeth
forgetting to breathe you into existence

and now the weight of March
lies heavy on my tongue
and it just seems too much like penance
while this thorny crown
digs it's claws into the world
not to say
every word
that my throat holds back

there is only the present left
and she ages by the second

PLEASE DON'T LET US BECOME SOME KIND OF TRAGEDY

We stood on our separate balconies
long before the mandates
of social distancing
trended upon our lips

when the only thing
lurking in the corners of our mouths
was the fact
we were still chewing
on all the poisoned I love yous
masquerading as goodbyes

all the wherefore art thous
stifled by pride

but all this seems so trivial
now that one simple gesture
of being human
could cancel all the words we have left

so I am here Romeo
calling for you
loudly.

I'VE TRIED TO KEEP THE WORDS IN BUT THEY WANT OUT

I tried to write a poem about you
but the words hung from my tongue
a clumped morass of uncertainty
so I swallowed them
and now all your adjectives
have lodged themselves in my stomach
and started to burn,
the smoky letters of your name
returning to my lips
so I can cough them into a poem.

as sun has kissed the darkened hills
at ending of the dying day
the birds they give their evening trills
as sun has kissed the darkened hills
with blush in pink and purple frills
the sea goes out from blue to gray
as sun has kissed the darkened hills
at ending of the dying day

WHILE WE WAIT (INSPIRED BY THE PAINTING – RENTAL SKIFFS, WILLOUGHBY SPIT BY JOHN GILBERT)

The beach is closed, the boats up on the sand
are circled by the birds, all footprints gone
and as the sun goes down the flames are fanned
and lick the waves, another day now done
as quiet hangs in air, without some words
or laughter on the wind, it all has stilled
the only chatter on the breeze are birds
and sea, as on to sand its song is spilled.
This sun sinks low, the purple tendrils hang
and paint the boats a vivid wash of dusk
and on the last of day there is a tang
of salt and life, now curled into a husk.
We will awaken slowly, soon with care
to boats and sea and birds, they are still there.

HOW I KNOW YOU LOVE ME IN THE MIDDLE OF MADNESS

we have stumbled
to knees
unused to prayers
our faces forgetting
the imprint of each other's lips
and grief
has torn holes
in all our excuses
in all our differences

but we can hear
each other's voices hanging
across all these empty gaps
in the stars between our hands

and despite all the mirages
and masks
that haunt us now
we still
know love

my hands slough poetry
like dead skin,
all those yesterdays
between my fingers
in twenty second washes
of words

i forget
that i am uncovering
sentences i last spoke
on rainy Tuesdays

your heart tasted bitter
i think i recall,
the menu of our everyday
life

but you were a taste

i think i still savour
flavours of us
on the edges of my tongue
when i'm alone
and there is nothing left to think of
but you

ALL OUR BROKEN PIECES WERE GLUED INTO A PHOTOGRAPH

we were broken
and we didn't realise
that there could be so many cuts
from fractured pieces
of past love affairs
and past hurts
still sharp in our throats

that when i said your name
the names of all the flesh
i had touched
that had already branded the tones of my skin
left so little room
to tattoo your fingerprints
into my flesh

but I can find those whorls of you
in the small of my back
dusted into the curves of my neck
find you on my tongue

i didn't promise to be
perfect
or a canvas for your words
but the only poem
my eyes imprinted
was the ocean of your chest

i didn't promise to be perfect
but then neither did you

My Pocket's Full Of Holes, But It Feels Like Someone's Sewn Rocks In The Hems Of My Jeans

i
i put you in my left front pocket;
you wore a hole
through to my skin
and left burn marks
all over
the landscape of my thighs

ii
i wrote you poetry;
the words
cascaded from the page
before i could get them to tell you
how i felt,
melted like a raging candle
burning through the last lengths
of its wick,
sputtered
and died

iii
i swore off love and left it in a corner;
i kept walking by
looking at all the dust
and neglect
but somehow couldn't clean it up,
so i let the spiders
call love home
call love theirs

iv
i picked up love to read a chapter;
i realized i hadn't read you
all the way to the end,
wondered
if that was deliberate
or if it was because you got bored
of our book club
after you'd dogeared choice sentences
took them out of context
and decided we were a metaphor
you didn't want to decipher.
i'm still intrigued
but wondering
if this thing will end in a cliffhanger

v
i wear a mask now, hoping my eyes bridge social distances;
i've been guarded
weighted
too tired to emote.
if i asked you
to lend me a glance
i often wonder
if you'd even hear me
over the silence

across tops
of skeletal sun dried branches
last leaves pointing to the ground
there, along a hill topped vista
one looming cloud, promising

spring cleaning
leaves are flicked
from desiccated gutters...
they will overflow with children's laughter
when hurricane season drips from the roof

the earliest recorded depression
forms in sister Pacific
as hot seas usher in summer
before summer
as Atlantic islands
hunker under lockdown skies
watching horizons
swallowing last years complacency
and hoarding hurricane supplies
without a breeze
in sight

i
there are no feet
to shuffle city dust;
it lies thick here
in the dark hushed tones
of Bourbon Street

ii
if i could sing
one drawn poetic note
would it bounce of the burnt hulk
of Gaiety
and resound in the foothills
of Marchand's sprawling skirts?
will anyone hear it?

iii
rats lay claim
to footprints,
to the last of us

WE CAN ONLY SEE EACH OTHER'S EYES FROM SIX FEET AWAY

Sahara dust chokes island skies
comes in a swath
tracked by satellite warnings
carried on Trades

we keep lying in the path
raising our hands
and asking
why the trash of our breaths
keeps floating
keeps sargassum
coming in on the tide

and through haze
we wonder
when we lost sight
of each other's faces
when we lost sight
of what we truly meant
to one another

now we are looking over gates
and fences
hoping that one day
we can take each other
for granted
and mean it

MY HANDS FEAR THE DEATH ON MY FACE

i decontaminate
the way you'd imagine
a heroine in a big screen movie
after she comes into alien contact
steps into that white shower tube
then stands under
hot pulsating strands of water
as if peeling the very air
from skin
that walked abroad

i flay fear
with soapy
thoughts

i strip
right
down
here
in all this naked
anxiety
my hands
stranded
and away from my face

a sonnet, love, a poem to confess
how butterflies have choked my very throat
and brought my tongue to state of sheer undress
how you are every word I ever wrote
and that cliches are now my solemn friends
they say they aren't but whisper neath the words
and I can see them draining from my pens
and hear them in the laughter of the birds.
I have to find some other way to couch
these sentences so that you'll find them whole
and not let all the letters groan and slouch
or else you may decide this love too droll.
perhaps I should say simply that I love
and give cliches the slip, the fall, a shove.

you show up in the blue mask
i hand pressed for you,
its folds against
lips i cannot see;
my hands scored lines
before the heat
etched protection into cotton,
etched a cloak
against lip read prayers
that haven't been there
in a decade

this disease
did not define our dysfunction;
we were hiding love
behind walls
long before its barbs
shut down all borders
between our flesh

we haven't touched each other
in a while
                    so why can't i breathe?
yet i know
the imprinted feel
of your flesh
in whorls of fingertips
identified
as yours;
they are used to social distancing

i have put your name
on a poem
placed it in my pocket
and called you close

they say the early signs of hypoxia
are anxiety
confusion
restlessness;
i've been breathing in
carbon dioxide
masquerading as feelings,
no wonder i am sick

love
is a heavy viral load,
you
are antibodies
fighting
flowing
living
beneath my skin

The clouds are choked with thick Saharan dust
a smothered cotton sky that hugs the hills
a muted tone that sunset turns to rust
and hushes all the throaty birdie trills
they're muffled like the sky, St.Lucian blue
cerulean, then tampered down to grey
and I am mesmerized by every hue
that flashes 'cross the faces of the day.
But these clouds now they promise but hold back
the rain we need, May festers dry and cracked
and I'll take skies that seem to have no knack
for torrents, than a hurricane's fierce act.
The rains will come, the skies hold clouds of black
when June first marks the start of every track.

I Hope The Prayers Were Heard, Even Faintly

Three children died over the last two months
all drowned, ages seven, fourteen, twenty one

they didn't stay in isolation, coaxed out by the
hot dry Saharan skies; these boys made their

mother's faces into masks at funerals that
ten or less could attend. Does it mean if

there were less attendees, offered prayers
were just a faint whisper? As waters gurgled,

rushing rivers, and one dark blue sea, like
a coolness their skins would soon become

a nation on hold could not mourn, could
not send wailers to the sides of sandy mounds

but kept on sleeping. And in judgement we
all asked why they weren't at home, and

let shelter in place orders shield our children
from the fatality that is living, a little longer.

IS IT THE BEGINNING OR THE ENDING OF THE CALL THAT HURTS MOST?

when you call
my smile breaks like wind
rancid on my face
even though you can't smell
forever on my breath
anymore

i want you to

weakness is a phantom
at the end of the phone

you still sound like yourself

i am some simpering old maid
                    i can hear it
dripping from my skin
a sepia image of the last time
your tongue
talked in code to my thighs

there is always air between
wanting
and needing

always a breath
with your name on it
that you only hear as

hi

I ONLY REMEMBER HER EYES

my grandmother's alcoholism
lived in a dark, one bedroom flat
in Kent, lived in her nurse's scrubs
lived on the clinking bottles that
littered red carpeted muffles
for her midnight treks from
bed to glass, her pilgrimage
wearing a path

it finally settled
in the blackened edges of
her breath, in fluttered
lashes plastered to her binge
full lips. settled in my
unheard sobs, small hands
shaking awake stupor
small hands that couldn't hold
her laugh

she didn't stay
long

these islands bury lots of broken bones
that hurricanes have snapped and left for done
and covered over with the toppled stones
that weigh upon the ground, that weigh a tonne
of screams the ground has swallowed, thick red dirt
cascaded down these hills and left deep scars
and trees have sprouted from the very hurt
beneath this canopy of shooting stars.
a litany of names, we know them all
from Dean, Tomas and Debbie, heard them roar
of Allen, Irma, Dorian, they maul
these lands are ripped apart from shore to shore.
the season starts anew, we hold our breath
we pray each track will change and spare us death

we pray each track will change and spare us death
and sometimes prayers are heard and sometimes not
from Cuba down the arc, the very breadth
the islands are one unity, one thought
as waves roll in across Atlantic surge
we watch and hope that Mother Nature's blast
will be a softer one this year, not scourge
like we have grappled with in years gone past.
a Caribbean people, we are strong
from Trinidad to Cuba, hear us sing
above the boom of wind and wave, lifelong
we thrive upon the rocks to which we cling.
we will outlive the tumble of each stone
these islands bury lots of broken bones

THE LIFE CYCLE OF A VIRUS

i
rain is coming.
thirty two days without a case
and we love our complacency,
our unmasked breaths
hanging in humidity,
our pillows
holding first drenches of sweat;
rain
is coming.

ii
Saharan dust
will be swept away
when hurricane eyes
lay sight on these islands.
our children
may have to stumble
into virus enfolding shelters;
the rain
will come wide in.

iii
when
this season
lays its final breath
along the neck of the archipelago,
the islands staggering once more
to bloodied feet,
will a crown of thorns
bloody our brows too?

iv
new leaves
green
will come from this land,
have to come
please
come
or we will be eating
the same dirt
for an eternity,
just waiting
for another hurricane season.

v
dogs are howling;
we have swatted death
closed our borders,
watched the Martinique channel
roil in indignation,
watched the pelicans
come back to human
silence;
but
the rains
are
coming.

vi
Yesterday, vagrancy touched my shoulder, asked me for
money from a schizophrenic memory. I recoiled in
revulsion from all the unknown viral death on her hands,
bit my guilt until my tongue bled. I am unworthy. The rains
are coming.

it's not

as if it isn't glaring
or that strange fruit hasn't hung
or that dark skin hasn't suffered
or that the sky is not the same from every angle

this skin is not an optical illusion in not being seen

shadows upon shadows
how words are stranded on lips

and now we have a list of names
but we have to do more
than just say them
Botham
George
Trayvon
Breonna

let us formulate a legacy
that is more than bones

more than the apology

my skin whispers to itself

last breaths
called every mother's name
black lives matter

love lives on the corner of your mouth
got dressed this morning
in Saharan dust grey
tried to say my name
caught on the soot on your tongue
teetered in the wind
and let another day
wind itself into a ball

love lives on the corner of your mouth
but hides behind a mask
with your smile
and your eyes aren't loud enough

love lives on the corner of your mouth

but you just can't name it

I think you're afraid
that it's deafening

THERE'S SO MUCH SMOG I MISSED IT WHEN YOU PUT YOUR SHOES ON

the horizon of your smile is plump with Saharan dust
i can barely see it in this light; the faint earthy curve
of your fingers now a mystery, mine can only lust for
tips searching through sandy deposits of your name preserved
in my mouth; my name once lived on your tongue
like a poem, a love letter, a spinal nerve

sending signals of the taste of me straight to your lungs
you coughed me out, stale exhale buried in the wind

WE ARE SO QUIET ABOUT IT, IT'S LIKE IT DOESN'T EXIST

this love
sits on the floor
between us
pools into droplets
circles contracting
while we watch
it evaporate
s l o w l y
our tongues
blind

I Swear I Just Looked Away For One Second

i don't know when you became a poem

maybe you have always been
a crowd of sentences
in the back of my throat
lined up
bus stop straight
waiting
to board the sorrow
we'd create

i don't know
when
i reduced our lives to words

but i did

THE ALCOHOL ON HER BREATH TOLD HER LIES

last year
i was the same age
that hung in my grandmother's throat
when she died

same age
of rum bottled promises
her tongue
could no longer wring out

same

outside has become heavy

when i get home
i strip the people from my flesh
watch the residue
of humanity
swirl down the drain

when did human touch
become a parody for death?
a breath
a laugh
something i step sideways off a sidewalk to avoid?

i come home
and i de-people
uncouple
leave you
in my social distance

my daughter
assembles my errant pieces
daily breathes me
into existence
calls it living
a fluid
un-thought of being

all my jagged edges
strain
accept
and call it
love

the edge of August
fades into September
spits dew onto early morning grass
until the sunburn of another day
sucks dry the offering

the air
seems to wait for permission
to break across hills
dust has claimed
from sight's memory

and grackles
mock everyone from wires
swaying
waiting for the exhaustion
of the setting sun
crawling into ocean's cradle at day's end

this country
seems to be waiting
for the world's eye
to reopen
and acknowledge that we still exist

do we even matter?

as hurricanes have sucked away
all breezes from the waiting land
the roses have all lost their sway
as hurricanes have sucked away
the every breath from every bay
red petals droop right where they stand
as hurricanes have sucked away
all breezes from the waiting land

one note
is always how we begin
and build to clattering crescendos
stacking ourselves
bone and breath intertwining

play me one note
add in the vibrato of pain
and I will collapse like leaves facing autumn
collapse
like waves facing formidable shores
collapse
like my sight against your turned cheek

play me one solitary note
love
love
love
I will know the beginning to the song
but never an ending

one
note
a defining echo
starts this song
and then simply
fades

my mouth is full of love poems

so stuffed, I can barely get the words out

seems ironic, when love doesn't know me
flung my name
over the back of a wingback chair
strewn with yesterday's clothes
crumpled and forgotten
in a corner

no one's been by
to shake out the folds
wonder if the creases are too much
to make it worth wearing
to inhale the fabric
see if it's stale   or still a little fresh round the edges

do you remember where you tossed me?

love?

these poems shudder
in my dry throat
crack
and dribble out of my lips
onto the floor

YOU MAKE ME SO BREATHLESS I FORGET WORDS

my tongue
searches for language
stutters and forgets syntax,
sentences

there are no words
a poem can chew,
spew
that add up to you

the clock
cannot dull the edges of this grief
its sonorous ticks
a requiem to everyday life

existence moves within the absence
slower than agreed
the edges of your name
always in the corners of the room
always on my tongue

i whisper morning hellos
into silence
say you into prayer

time it seems cannot bend love to its will
and make it less
for grief is only a negative image
of love's shroud

and I cloak myself here
in the seconds

WE TALK ABOUT HOPE WHILE CLINGING TO DARKNESS

March 11, 2020
the first cloth mask
rolls from my mother's industrial fingers,
white strings flapping surrender

it is my birthday
the day the announcement
infects the television screen
in the small wooden rumshop
where my girlfriends and i
raise quaking glasses to another year

i spend months
ironing folds into conversations
with small hopes

keep glued
to screens
where my phone beeps five minute
conspiracy theories

and watch death clocks
toll daily numbers

my daughter's eyes
show strain
when she asks if her newly minted boyfriend
can come watch the year
drag its final steps
into our living room
where our Christmas tree will soon huddle,

asks whether his fingers
can help her reach the top and place the angel

and i have to say the loudest word
that this year has built
brick by sentenced brick
along my wearied tongue

no.

FROM UNDER EVERY POEM YOUR NAME PEEKS OUT

i thought i'd forgotten how to write you a love poem

this year has dragged my poetic intentions
in directions
my fingers stumble to walk,
words outstretched like toddlers
tasting freedom

i have teetered in my run
thought every skinned knee was a learning curve
thought i was finally learning to breathe
more than your name

but i should have realized by now
you are DNA entangled
in the pocket of my jeans

you are every cool sip
of warm peppermint tea
on a too hot afternoon,
when the sweat
pools in the cradles of my clavicles

and you
are poetry
i have yet to write

i try to stay asleep
because you are always
on the periphery
that corner of the eye ghost
working out subconscious equations
of whether or not this world
could ever support
all the bitter taste of what we are in daylight

(you are always sweet when i'm unconscious)

i draw you in
breathe poetry
so that my hands scramble for black penned pages
write
lyrics
on my exhales

but my bed looks like a kidnapped crime scene
because you're never in it

only the dawn
scratches my eyelids
clawing me into the bloodbath of words
i dreamt last night

until i tire of dreams

I FILTER YOUR WORDS THROUGH THE CAR SPEAKERS
SO I CAN CALL IT LOVE

bubble-wrapped sentiment
in phone call circles
you say
the right sentences

i pluck at packaging
cushioned from cuts

labelling pain
love

return to sender

DAMN THIS ONE NOTE SERENADE, YOU'RE NOT EVEN LISTENING TO

i wonder if i would write poetry anymore
if your voice
wasn't like an ocean in my inner ear,
a crashing wave on my tongue

maybe the words would drown
into banal sentences
and i wouldn't feel the urge
to try and immortalize
all the language we exchange

there's no such thing as writer's block apparently;
when i don't write for a while
my heart bangs into my ribs
until i can't breathe,
the dam of words
flooding the spillway of my mouth

sometimes
just for a moment
i wonder what it would be like
to be silent

what it would be like
to forget
your name

IS THIS ENOUGH, WHEN I'M CHOKING ON MORE?

we are sprawled out Sundays
our knees warming the one inch gap
between them
our fingers brushing sentences
our mouths cannot utter

> *i love you*
> *is an implied construct*
> *behind our eyes*
> *where pain breathes*
> *on the ashes of all we've ever said*

and keeps them
faintly   glowing

FUCK YOU FOR NOT CARING, LOVE'S DEAD ANYWAY

my body has been colonized by pain,
it set up camp in my ribs
tent posts slammed in tight
to the interstices of each breath
so long ago
that my lungs only know how to sip
instead of gulp

i have tasted you
like iron on my tongue
like rust;
i'm afraid it will crack if i move

i am a stagnant pond
covered in algae's breath
a contamination of poetry
that never changes

i think i have forgotten what it means to be whole

and if this is what death looks like
on a random Monday in January
i'm not sure
i've been living

I KNOW THIS IS JUST A POEM.....RIGHT?

i can feel myself
all damp paper edges
folding along the crease of your smile

i say glib things
            "*whatever you need*"
without revealing how much i need
to wrap my fingers in the palm of your hand
and pretend they mean   sorry

i am all love crushed
damaged corners
and trampled heartbeats
beating in stammers

you probably think i'm easy
instead of recognizing the addict in my answers,
i haven't smoked a cigarette in twenty five years
but that doesn't mean
i don't crave stained fingers

i still think you live in the lobes of my lungs

i cough you into bent elbows
like i've been taught
and i try
man, do i hold myself back
from just saying

hold me

in the wind dropped stillness
a chirp of tree frogs takes up notes
cool air sinks through the screen door
slinks in with night on its heels
drops to my feet
and stays a while

and then the breeze
rustles through the browning split lip leaves
of the banana trees
propped up
in their drunken birthing

nudges the dogs
to roll call across the hills
"are you there?"

smell of sickly sweet campeche
blooms its hot yellow in the dark
clings to the back of throats
to tongues
gossiping in curfewed tones
from balconies

this land has never been so still
so quiet
that you can hear stars ripen
and fall
like mangoes thudding to the earth
plump in the moonlight

this is what waiting tastes like

Her Voice Went Quiet And Settled In My Ribs

my grandmother's voice
crawled out of a bottle every morning
hustled out by the empty clink
of rattled glass
feet stumbling last night's dance
onto the deep red carpet

boomed out into the shop
over my six year old head
pushing over queued patrons

somehow i knew
even through the embarrassed hunch
of my small shoulders
that the amplified megaphone of her twisted thought
could thump into the air
and echo like a slap

and then
over some purple Easter
her voice rolled out of the last bottle
sat in her liver
and went quiet

fifty two

that number is a mantra
my bones know
the number of prayers
my stomach coughs up into my throat
when the littered ghost of that red carpet
floats through my teeth

but i'm not sure
that she hears my litany
hears the crack in my ribs
that carved itself
deep on that purple Easter

hears the hitch in my voice
when i try to give her name life

THIS BOOK IS UNFINISHED BECAUSE I DON'T KNOW IF I WILL LIKE THE ENDING

i can brush your hand
(with a poem)
stare out loud at your mouth
(so loud that the words curl at the edges!)
we are fast paced
(WhatsApp messages)

i am scared

that all i am
is this poem
that my vocal chords know your name
but have forgotten how to annunciate the syllables

that i live
only in the crumpled up
thrown away, red-lined mistakes
shaking, handwritten
things

sometimes i hate
what we've become

sometimes
i think
we can't be anything else

THE LEAVING AFFAIR

i.
my grandmother's second husband loved her.
he wasn't the serial marrying kind like my grandfather
he stayed as long as he could
until the rum she had transported
in her veins from the island
liquefied between them,
the dreary drip of cold grey English skies
lost in bottles
she cradled to forget

ii
my father tells the story of arriving on a train platform
banana boat sickness still in his gut
the last vestiges of St. Lucian soil clinging to his shoes
watching her trying to find the baby
she abandoned to her mother's hands
his sixteen year old eyes
suddenly more mature in the knowing
of who she was
what she had become

iii
she had a love affair with a bottle
and didn't know how to beat the obsession
even dressed tight in her nurse's uniform
she did not see the irony
of administering hope
when she could not comprehend what hope was

iv
love is sometimes the story of leaving

v
and so she left
hooked up to machines
far too early
and too much in love

I Talk A Good Game, But I Don't Mean A Word

i breathe you in
all Saharan dust cloudy
smoky tones and coal fire ash

i am lungs on fire
teeth biting down on a tongue
so your name won't escape

there is a chasm
between our sentences
they are nothing on repeat

we forgot how to listen
when we left each other
so now we pretend in two dimensional limbo

i wish i had the courage to recite poetry

i fail in the English language to be more than banal
i am afraid of rejection
so does that mean i'm human?

does that mean you love me?
it is possible to read anything into the word "hello"

i left my real voice in the back pocket of your jeans
when you sauntered out the door

i want it back

the wind has brought your scent in through the door
a tease, my mind gets drunk and breathes you in
your eyes they trigger stutters, nothing more
makes sense, and I am anxious in my skin
too scared to say your name, to whisper hope
into the room, I close my eyes instead
and try to steady breathing, try to cope
with all the swirling thoughts inside my head

your smile it knows, it sees my heated blush
my flesh betrays me, fingers tremble, clench
to keep the words from coming in a rush
there's not enough to give this thirst its quench

you know I love, it's painted on my face
and I am left a mess, devoid of grace

my great grandmother had six daughters and one son.
five of her daughters
were all baptized with the name Anne Marie
including the twins,
so they all gathered the house names
she collectively christened them with
because the parish priest could not lift his pen
long enough out of the well of her illiteracy
to be creative,
except for the last born daughter
for whom it seemed there were no ancestral names
left on my great grandmother's tongue to pass on,
and Anne Marie took her baptismal name to her grave
long after all her other sisters
had taken their last breaths

all but my grandmother
who for some reason
must have been particularly warranting
a name of her own,
evidenced by her own consonants and vowels
typed in black letters
on my father's baptism and birth certificate
her name etched besides the word MOTHER
OCCUPATION…Labourer

my great grandmother's son
was killed at seventeen in a freak accident,
I think his sisters split his name on their tongues
I think my grandmother spent her days
trying to drown the syllables with drink

maybe my grandmother left my father
for sixteen years with her mother

as substitute
as offering,
but he would never know the extent of her name
beyond the walls of the bottle he found her in
when his feet finally managed to be
in the same place as hers

three of the Anne Marie's died of dementia
forgetting the syllables of their stories

I guess the rest of us left
must remember to say their blessing names
so the years do not swallow them whole
and spit them into one person,
so that they are more than pieces of paper
in a dusty parish record.

YOU NEVER LEFT, DID YOU?

sometimes you claim space
as if you never left the orbit of my ribs
calm in assertions
that all will be the same

i let you get away with it
because ghostly whispers of you
are still in my bed
and the sheets pile into sepia imprints
in moonlight mirages

The Flip Side Is You Don't Notice, So I Guess We're Good

when you walk out of the room

you take the edges of my last breath,
contrails following you to the door

my smile shatters,
teeth leaning like time worn henges

this is when my mask becomes a shield

my world turns 12 am
and the only sound is a treefrog chorus

i don't think i can stay numb
like this
forever

www.ingramcontent.com/pod-product-compliance
Lightning Source LLC
Chambersburg PA
CBHW060426090426
42734CB00011B/2462